Student Interactive

myView
LITERACY

K

SAVVAS
LEARNING COMPANY

ISBN-13: 978-0-134-90869-4
ISBN-10: 0-134-90869-4

14 2023

Julie Coiro, Ph.D.

Jim Cummins, Ph.D.

Pat Cunningham, Ph.D.

Elfrieda Hiebert, Ph.D.

Pamela Mason, Ed.D.

Ernest Morrell, Ph.D.

P. David Pearson, Ph.D.

Frank Serafini, Ph.D.

Alfred Tatum, Ph.D.

Sharon Vaughn, Ph.D.

Judy Wallis, Ed.D.

Lee Wright, Ed.D.

Going Places

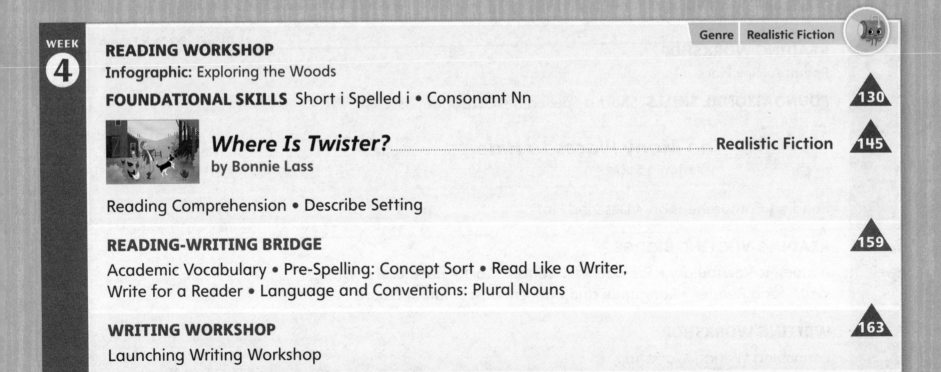

Going Places

Essential Question

What makes a place special?

 Watch

"**My Community**" and see what you can learn about special places.

 TURN and TALK

What places are in your community?

SAVVAS realize™

Go ONLINE for all lessons.

 VIDEO

 AUDIO

 GAME

 ANNOTATE

 BOOK

RESEARCH

Spotlight on Realistic Fiction

Reading Workshop

Reading-Writing Bridge

• Academic Vocabulary • Pre-Spelling • Read Like a
Writer, Write for a Reader • Language and Conventions

Writing Workshop

• Independent Writing and Conferences • Meet the Author • When to Start a New Book
• Make and Respond to Suggestions • Publish and Celebrate

Project-Based Inquiry

• Inquire • Research • Collaborate

Independent Reading

You can learn to be a good reader!

1. Choose a book.

2. Hold it right side up.

3. Start at the front cover.

4. Turn the pages carefully.

Directions Discuss the steps for reading with students. Say: Pick a book that looks interesting. Look through the book to make sure it is not too easy or too hard. Show a book and model how to identify the front cover, back cover, and title page. Then model how to hold the book right side up and turn pages correctly. Finally, model how to read from left to right and from top to bottom, including return sweep.

My Independent Reading Log

Date	Book	Pages Read	My Ratings
			😊 😐 ☹️
			😊 😐 ☹️
			😊 😐 ☹️
			😊 😐 ☹️

Directions Have students self-select a text to read independently. Ask them to identify the front cover, back cover, and title page of the book. Then ask them to read the book correctly by holding it right side up and turning the pages carefully as they read from left to right and from top to bottom. Finally, have students complete the chart to tell about their independent reading.

11

Unit Goals

In this unit, you will

○ read fiction texts

△ draw or write a text

☐ talk about what makes a place special

 **MY TURN** Color

Directions Read aloud the unit goals to students. Then ask them to identify the place in the picture and talk about what makes the place special. Have students color the picture.

Academic Vocabulary

map	move	land	special

A park is a **special** place. 👍 👎

It is fun to **move** to a new place. 👍 👎

A **map** is a helpful tool. 👍 👎

I like to plant things in the **land**. 👍 👎

TURN and TALK Talk about your answers.

Directions Read aloud the Academic Vocabulary words and the sentences to students. Have students color the thumbs up if they agree with the statement and the thumbs down if they do not agree. Then have students use the newly acquired Academic Vocabulary to talk about their responses with a partner.

Read Together

Using Your Imagination

You can use your imagination when you play.

14

Weekly Question

How does imagination make a place seem different?

You can write about the places you imagine.

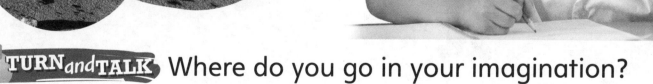 **TURN and TALK** Where do you go in your imagination?

Directions Read the text to students. Then have them interact with the source by looking at the pictures and text and talking about how they can use their imaginations to go places.

 15

Initial Sounds

 Circle

Directions Have students circle the picture word in each pair that begins with the sound /m/. Model: Listen to the beginning sounds in these words: /m/ -ouse, /k/ -at. The word *mouse* begins with the sound /m/.

Consonant Mm

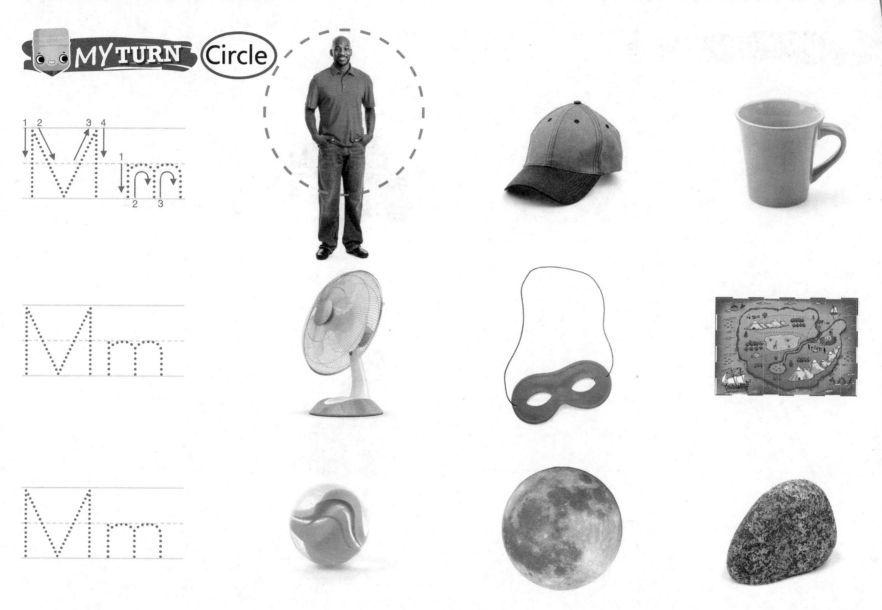

Directions Tell students that the letter *m* can make the sound /m/. Model how to form the letters *M* and *m*. Say: You will see the letter *m* in many words that have the sound /m/. Trace the letters *Mm*. Point to the letter *m* and identify, or tell me, the sound it makes. Now you will match the letters and the sound. Circle each picture that has the sound for *m* at the beginning.

17

Consonant Mm

 Write

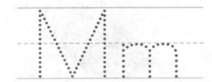

Directions Have students say each picture word and identify the beginning sound. Say: If the word begins with the sound /m/, write the letters *Mm* on the lines.

Initial and Final Sounds

 Circle

Directions Say: Listen to the sound at the beginning of this word: /t/ -ire. The beginning sound is /t/. Have students circle the picture words in the first row that begin with the same sound as *tire* and the picture words in the second row that end with the same sound as *pot*.

Consonant Tt

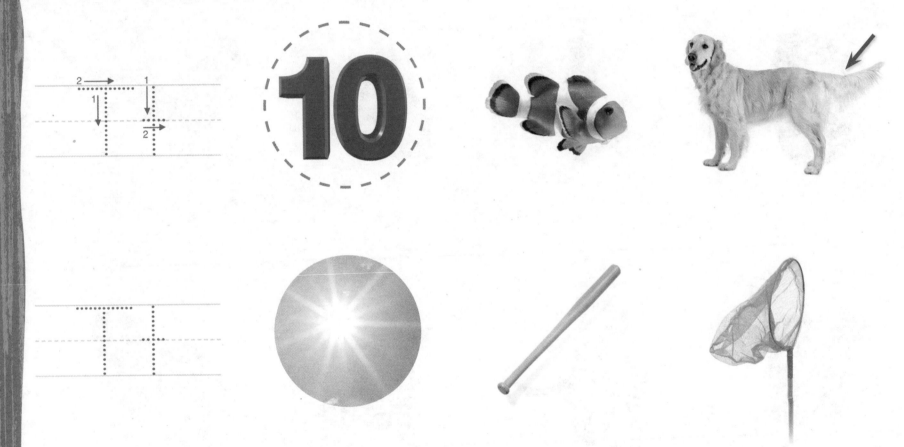

Directions Tell students that the letter *t* can make the sound /t/. Say: You will see the letter *t* in many words that have the sound /t/. Model how to form the letters *T* and *t*. Have students trace the letters *Tt* and identify the sound that *t* makes. Then have them match the letters and sound by circling the picture words in the first row that begin with the sound for *t* and the picture words in the second row that end with the sound for *t*.

My Words to Know

I	am	the

My Sentences to Read

I am the .

I am the .

Directions Say: There are some words we will see a lot when we read. Listen as I read these words: *I, am, the.* Have students read the high-frequency words. Then say: You can identify, or find, the words in sentences. Ask students to look at the sentences and underline the high-frequency words. Then have them read the sentences, using the words *mouse* and *lion* to name the images.

21

Consonant Tt

 MY TURN Write

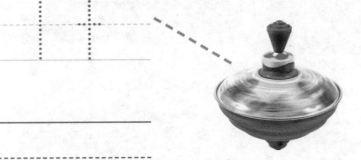

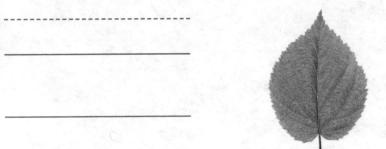

22

Directions Say: Remember that the letter *t* makes the sound /t/. Have students write the letters *Tt* on the lines and identify the sound that *t* makes. Then have them draw lines to match the letters to the picture words that begin or end with the sound for *t*.

I Am

Highlight the word with the **m** sound and the picture whose name begins with the **m** sound.

I am the .

 AUDIO
Audio with Highlighting

 ANNOTATE

23

I am the .

I am the  .

24

Underline the pictures whose names begin with the **t** sound.

I am the .

25

Consonants Mm and Tt

 MY TURN Write and read

map

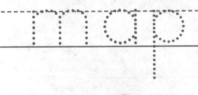

10

26

Directions Remind students that the letter *m* makes the sound /m/ and the letter *t* makes the sound /t/. Have students name each picture. Then have them write the word for the picture. Finally, have them read the words.

Consonants Mm and Tt

 **Circle**

I am the . （Mm） Tt

I am the . Mm Tt

I am the . Mm Tt

I am the . Mm Tt

Directions Have students read the sentences. Ask them to circle the letters that match the beginning sound of the animal name in each sentence.

Read Together

My Learning Goal

I can read realistic fiction.

SPOTLIGHT ON GENRE

Realistic Fiction

Realistic fiction is a story that could happen in real life.

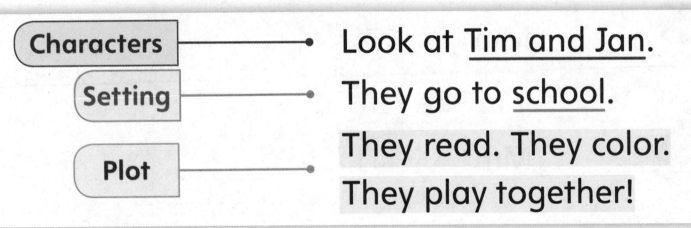

Characters ————• Look at <u>Tim and Jan</u>.

Setting ————• They go to <u>school</u>.

Plot ————• They read. They color.
They play together!

 TURN and TALK Talk about how you know this story is realistic fiction.

Directions Say: Characters are the people or animals in a story. Setting is where and when a story takes place. Plot is what happens, or the main events, in a story. Have students identify and describe the characters, setting, and plot in the model text. Then have them discuss how they know it is realistic fiction.

Realistic Fiction
Anchor Chart

Characters

Setting

Events

1

2

3

 **Read Together**

Mission Accomplished!

Preview Vocabulary

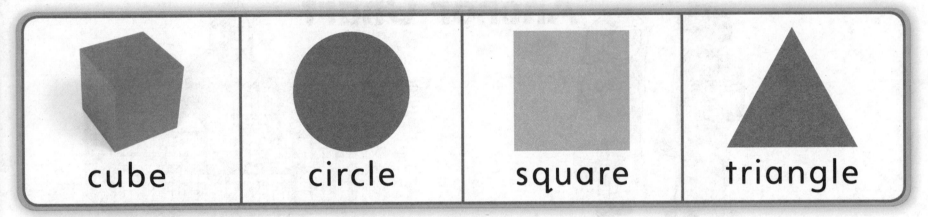

cube | circle | square | triangle

Read

Read the story to find out what the characters do.

Meet *the* Author

Ebony Joy Wilkins writes books for children and schools. She used to be a teacher. She likes traveling, playing tennis, and visiting her family.

Mission Accomplished!

written by Ebony Joy Wilkins

illustrated by Kevin Zimmer

 AUDIO

Audio with Highlighting

 ANNOTATE

31

Rena, we need more rocks!
Where can we find some?

CLOSE READ

Underline the name of the girl in the story.

I know where.
We can go to Mars.

33

Buckle up, Christopher.
Mars, here we come!

34

CLOSE READ

<u>Underline</u> the name of the boy in the story.

This rock is shaped like a cube.
I'll take it.

35

This rock is shaped like a circle.
I'll take it.

This rock is shaped like a square.
I'll take it.

This rock is shaped like a triangle.
But there's no room.

CLOSE READ

What word can you use to describe Rena and Christopher? Highlight words in the story that make you think this.

I have room.
Mission accomplished!
Let's go home.

Develop Vocabulary

 Match

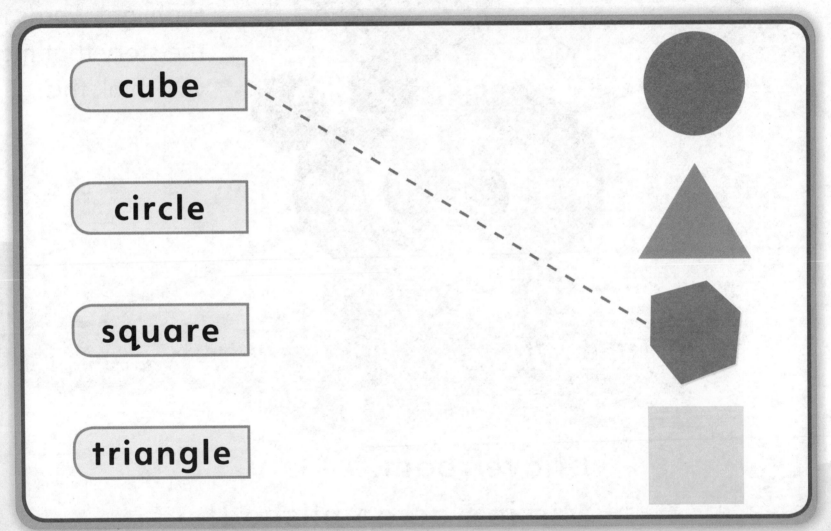

cube

circle

square

triangle

Directions Read the vocabulary words to students. Then have them use illustrations to clarify the meanings of the words by drawing a line from each word to the matching picture.

Check for Understanding

 **MY TURN** (Circle) and write

1. Where does the story happen?

park	home

2. Why does the author have the children go home?

_____

_____

_____

3. What do the children do?

_____

_____

_____

Directions Read question 1 and the answer choices aloud to students. Have them circle the answer. Then read questions 2 and 3 and have students write their answers.

Identify and Describe Characters

Characters are the people or animals in a story.

The **main characters** are who a story is mostly about.

 Write

_____

- -

_____

_____

- -

_____

Directions Read the information to students. Have them look back at the text and identify the main characters. Then have students write the characters' names next to their pictures.

Use Text Evidence

 Draw

Directions Say: You can use details, or evidence, in a story to tell about the characters. Have students describe the main characters by drawing pictures of them. Remind students to look back at the text. Encourage them to look for details about the characters to add to their pictures.

Reflect and Share

 Draw

Weekly Question

How does imagination make a place seem different?

44

Directions Tell students they read about characters who collect rocks together. Ask them to think of other characters they have read about. Have students respond to sources by drawing a picture of Rena or Christopher and a character from another story.

Read Together

I can use words to tell about stories.

My Learning Goal

Academic Vocabulary

map	move	land	special

 Circle and match

moves

remove

Directions Remind students that word parts can be added to words to make new words. Read each word and ask students to circle the word part that was added to the word *move*. Then have students draw a line from each word to the matching picture.

Concept Sort

 Circle

46

Directions Have students name the pictures and circle the picture words for animals. Then have students use the words to talk about the category. Ask: How are the circled picture words alike?

Read Like a Writer, Write for a Reader

 Write

1. Find two words in the story that help you picture what the rocks look like.

_____

- -

_____

2. What other word can you use to tell what a rock looks like?

_____

- -

_____

Directions Say: We can experience a story by picturing it in our minds. Authors use words that help readers visualize, or picture in their minds what is happening. Read aloud pp. 35–38 as students picture the events in their minds. Read the items and have students write and discuss their responses.

47

Singular Nouns

A **noun** can name a person or an animal.

girl

dog

 **TURN and TALK** Say other words you know that name a person or an animal.

MY TURN Write

cat	boy

_____

The _____ reads a book.

48

Directions Read the information at the top of the page and explain that a singular noun names each one. Have students talk with a partner about other nouns for people and animals. Then have students edit the sentence by writing the correct singular noun on the lines.

My Learning Goal

I can draw or write.

Introduction to Writing Workshop

Think about your favorite book.

Have you ever thought about who wrote it?

An **author** is someone who writes a book.

TURN and TALK Think like an author.

What books could you write?

You can be an author too!

Directions Have partners discuss their ideas about books they can write. Remind them to speak clearly as they share ideas with their partner.

49

What Good Writers Do

Writing Workshop will help you learn to be a good writer.

 Match

1. I will learn.

2. I will write.

3. I will talk.

4. I will share.

50

Directions Discuss with students how they should act during each part of the Writing Workshop. Read each sentence with students, and then have them draw lines from each part of the Writing Workshop to the appropriate action.

Independent Writing and Conferences

How will you write on your own?

Think of ideas. Choose an idea. Write about it!

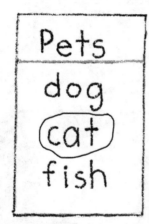

How will you talk about your writing?

☐ Ask questions. ☐ Listen actively.

☐ Share ideas. ☐ Stay on topic.

TURN and TALK Tell what you should do when you write on your own. Tell what you should do when you talk about your writing.

Directions Discuss with students what they are expected to do during independent writing and conferences. Then ask students to talk about what they should do during independent writing and conferences with a partner.

A New Place

I pack my toys and books.

Look at all that space!

I wonder what it will be like

To live in a new place.

old house

What is exciting about moving to a new place?

We pull up on the street,
And look at what we see!
Boys and girls are playing.
Will they be friends with me?

new house

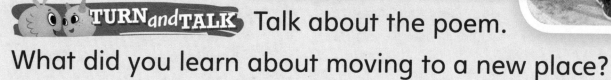 Talk about the poem.
What did you learn about moving to a new place?

Directions Read the poem to students. Then have them interact with the source by discussing how the author feels about moving to a new place and why. Ask students to tell what they learned about moving to a new place.

Middle Sounds

 SEE and SAY (Circle)

Directions Model: Listen to the sounds in *sack*: /s/ /a/ /k/. *Sack* has the sound /a/ in the middle. Have students say the sounds in each picture word and circle the ones with /a/ in the middle.

Short a Spelled a

 Circle

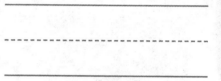

Directions Tell students that the letter *a* can make the sound /a/. Model how to form the letters *A* and *a*.
Then say: You will see the letter *a* in many words that have the short *a* sound. Point to the letter *a* and tell
me the sound it makes. Now say each picture word and circle the pictures that have the short *a* sound in the
middle. Write the letters *Aa* next to the pictures that have the short *a* sound.

55

Short a Spelled a

 Write

 map

 mat

 bat

56

Directions Have students trace the letter *a* in each word. Then ask them to identify and say the sounds for the letters they know in each word and write the letters on the lines. Finally, have students use the picture to identify and say each word.

Alliteration

 Underline

Directions Say: Some groups of words, such as *ant*, *ask*, and *apple*, begin with the same sound. Listen to this word: /s/-*un*, *sun*. Which picture words in the first row begin with the same sound as *sun*? Have students recognize spoken alliteration by underlining the picture words in the first row with the same initial sound. Continue with the second row.

57

Consonant Ss

MY TURN <u>Underline</u>

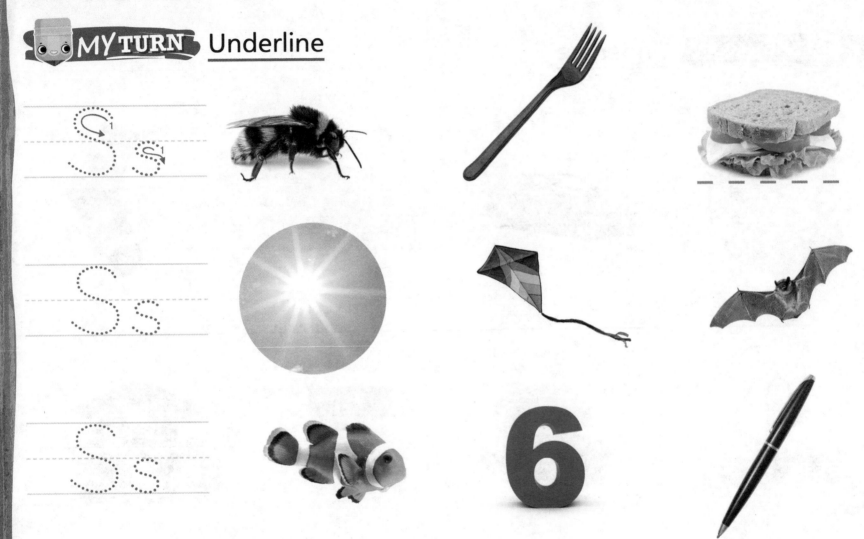

Directions Tell students that the letter s can make the sound /s/. Model how to form the letters S and s. Then say: You will see the letter s in many words that have the /s/ sound. Trace the letters Ss. Point to the letter s and tell me the sound it makes. Now underline the picture word in each row that begins with the sound for s.

My Words to Know

a	to	like

My Sentences to Read

I <u>like</u> to .

I like a 🥊.

Directions Model: There are some words we will see a lot when we read. Listen as I read these words: *a*, *to*, *like*. Have students read the high-frequency words. **Then say:** You can identify, or find, the words in sentences. Look at the sentences and underline the words *a*, *to*, and *like*. **Have students read the sentences, using the words *bat* and *mitt* to name the images.**

59

Consonant Ss

 MY TURN Read, match, and write

Sam - - - - - - - - - - - - - - - -

sat

_____

- -

_____

Directions Remind students that the letter *s* can make the sound /s/. Say: Use what you know about letters and sounds to read each word. Then draw a line from each word to the matching picture. (Tell students that the boy's name is Sam.) After students match the words to the pictures, have them choose one of the words to write on the lines.

Sam Sat

Highlight the words with the **s** sound.

I am Sam.

 AUDIO

Audio with Highlighting

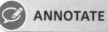 ANNOTATE

 61

I like to .

I like a m̲a̲t̲.

Underline the words with the short **a** sound.

Sam sat at the mat.

63

Short a and Consonant Ss

 Read

 **at**

 **am**

 **Sam**

 **sat**

64

Directions Remind students that the letter *s* can make the sound /s/ and that the letter *a* can make the sound /a/. Have students take turns decoding the VC and CVC words using letter-sound relationships. Say: Point to each letter in the word and say the sound it makes. Then say the sounds together to read the word.

Short a and Consonant Ss

 Circle and underline

I am Tam.

I like the .

I am Sam.

I like to 🧒 .

Directions Have students read the sentences, using letter-sound relationships to decode the VC and CVC words. Model: The sound for *a* is /a/. The sound for *m* is /m/. I will say the sounds together to read the word: /a/ /m/, *am*. Then have them circle the words or picture names with short *a* and underline the words or picture names with initial *s*.

Read Together

My Learning Goal

I can read realistic fiction.

SPOTLIGHT ON GENRE

Realistic Fiction

The **plot** is what happens in a story.

Problem

Resolution

TURN and TALK Talk about the problem and the resolution. What did the girl do?

66

Directions Read the information and remind students that a story has main events, or events that happen at the beginning, middle, and end. Say: A story also has a problem, or something that needs to be fixed, and a resolution, or how the problem is fixed. Have students describe the problem and resolution in the pictures.

Realistic Fiction Anchor Chart

Problem

Resolution

The pictures and words in a story tell what happens.

Read Together

Too Many Places to Hide

Preview Vocabulary

crawls	peeks	unpacks	plunks

Read

What questions do you have about this story?

Meet the Author

Antonio Sacre writes books, tells stories, and reads all the time. He has a cat that hides in his sock drawer.

Directions Say: You can ask questions about a story before you read it. Asking and answering questions before, during, and after reading can help you better understand a story and get information. Encourage students to look at the illustration on the title page and ask questions about the story before reading.

Too Many Places to Hide

written by Antonio Sacre ■ illustrated by Jaime Kim

AUDIO

Audio with Highlighting

ANNOTATE

We just moved from the city.
Boxes are everywhere,
and Poof is gone!

CLOSE READ

What is the problem? <u>Underline</u> the words that name the problem.

Dad said he saw her in the kitchen earlier. Poof is not there now!

Our new home has too
many places to hide!
How will we ever find Poof?

Mateo helps me look.
He crawls way back in the closet.
No Poof.

Mom helps me look.
She peeks under the couch.
No Poof.

CLOSE READ

What questions can you ask about what happens on these pages? Highlight the words that answer the questions.

Mateo unpacks bowls.
Dad plunks down cat food.
I have an idea!

75

Mateo hands me a bowl.
Dad helps me fill it with cat food.

76

CLOSE READ

How does the narrator find Poof? <u>Underline</u> the resolution.

Come, Poof!
Dinnertime!
Here is Poof!

Develop Vocabulary

crawls	peeks	unpacks	plunks

 Draw

Directions Read the vocabulary words to students. Then have them choose a word and draw a picture to show the meaning of the word.

Check for Understanding

 **MY TURN** (Circle) and write

1. The events   **could** | **could not**   really happen.

2. Why do you think the author wrote this text?

_____

- -

_____

3. Poof comes out because

_____

- -

_____ •

Directions Read item 1 and the answer choices aloud to students. Have them circle the answer. Then read items 2 and 3 and encourage students to write their responses. Remind them to use text evidence.

Describe Plot

 Draw

Problem ➡️ Resolution

80

Directions Say: A problem is something in a story that needs to be fixed. A resolution is how the problem is fixed. Have students draw pictures to describe the problem and resolution in the story. Remind them to look back at the text.

Ask and Answer Questions

You can ask questions to help you understand a story or get information.

You can use details in the story to answer your questions.

 **MY TURN** Draw

Directions Read the information about asking and answering questions. Have students look back at the text. Ask them to share a question they had during reading or think of a new question with a partner. Then have them draw the answer to their question using text details.

Reflect and Share

 **TURN and TALK** Tell about the problem and resolution in the story. How does this plot remind you of other stories you have read?

> You can retell the events in a story.

Weekly Question

What is exciting about moving to a new place?

82

Directions Tell students they read about characters who solve a problem. Have students retell the events in the story, including the problem and resolution. Say: When you retell a story, you tell the important events. Then have them respond to sources by talking about how the plot is similar to other stories they have read.

Read Together

I can use words to tell about stories.

My Learning Goal

Academic Vocabulary

map	move	land	special

 MY TURN (Circle) and underline

move

leave

stay

Directions Read the words to students. Ask them to circle the word that has a similar meaning to the word *move*. Have them underline the word that has the opposite meaning.

83

Concept Sort

 Match

84

Directions Have students identify the picture words on the left as *food* or *not food*. Then have them draw a line to match each picture word on the left to a picture word on the right that belongs in the same category.

Read Like a Writer, Write for a Reader

 Write

1. Who tells the story? Find words in the text
that help you know who tells the story.

_____

- -

_____

2. Write a sentence that tells about an event.
Use the word **I**.

_____

- -

_____

Directions Say: Sometimes a character is the narrator, or the person telling a story. The narrator uses words such
as _I_ and _we_ to tell the story. Have students listen to and experience first-person text as you read aloud a page
from the story. Then read the items one at a time and have students write their responses.

Singular Nouns

A **noun** can name a thing or a place.

ball  park

 Tell which word names a thing. Tell which word names a place.

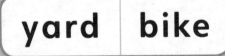 Write

| yard | bike |

The _____ is in the _____.

86

Directions Read the information at the top of the page. Have students identify which noun names a thing and which one names a place. Then have students edit the sentence by writing each singular noun in the correct position in the sentence.

Read
Together

WRITING WORKSHOP

I can draw or write.

My
Learning
Goal

Parts of a Book

Books have a front cover, a back cover, and a title page.

 Match

| front cover | back cover | title page |

Directions Say: The front cover names the title and author of a book. The title page is the first page in a book. It names the title and author too. The back cover tells details about a book. Ask students to identify the front cover, back cover, and title page by drawing a line from each term to the matching image.

Parts of a Page

A page has **words.** Words tell a story or information.

A page has **pictures.** Pictures show more about the words.

 Write and draw

Directions Display a book from the classroom library and explain how the author uses print and graphic features, including the main text and pictures, to achieve a specific purpose. Then encourage students to create a page for a book using both words and pictures.

Meet the Author

An **author** is the person who writes a book.

 Write and draw

_____

- -

_____

Directions Discuss the author's role in writing a book. Then encourage students to tell about themselves as authors by drawing and writing.

Read Together

National Parks

National parks are special places.
You might see interesting animals.

What makes us want to visit a special place?

You can hike.
What might you
see as you hike?

You can learn about the past.
People lived here long ago.

Talk to your partner about what makes national parks special.

Directions Read the text to students. Have them interact with the source by looking at the pictures and explaining why national parks are special places.

91

Sound Parts

 **Circle**

Directions Have students segment and blend the onset and rime in each picture word. Then have them circle the word in each pair that begins with the sound /p/. Model: Listen to this word: /p/-ig, pig. The word pig begins with the sound /p/.

Consonant Pp

 Write

Directions Tell students that the letter *p* stands for the sound /p/. Explain that they will see the letter *p* in many words that begin with the sound /p/. Model how to form the letters *P* and *p*. Then have students say the name of each picture and tell whether the picture word starts with *p*. Say: If the picture word starts with *p*, write the letters. If the picture word does not start with *p*, draw an X over the picture.

93

Consonant Pp

 **MY TURN** Read and write

tap

map

Pam

Directions Have students name the first picture and tell what letter the picture word ends with. Then ask them to trace the letter in the word. Finally, have students read the word and write it on the lines. Repeat with the remaining pictures and words.

Sound Parts

 Circle

Directions Name the pictures in the first row with students. Model segmenting and blending onset and rime: Listen to this word: /k/-*an, can.* Have students segment and blend the onset and rime in the remaining words and circle the picture words that start with /k/. Then have them continue with the second row.

Consonant Cc

 MY TURN (Circle)

96

Directions Tell students that the letter c can make the sound /k/. Model how to form the letters C and c. Say: You will see the letter c in many words that begin with the sound /k/. Trace the letters Cc. Point to the letters and say the sound they can make. Now circle each picture word that begins with the sound for c.

My Words to Know

he	is	have

My Sentences to Read

He is a cat.

I have a map.

Directions Listen as I read these words: *he, is, have.* Have students read the words in the word bank as they point to each word. Then have them read the sentences with you and underline the high-frequency words.

Consonant Cc

  Read and match

 cap

 Cam

cat

 98

Directions Have students trace the letter C or c in each word. Then have them decode the words. Finally, have students draw a line from each word to the matching picture.

The Map

I have a cat.

He is Mac.

 AUDIO

Audio with Highlighting

 ANNOTATE

99

I pat Mac.

Underline the words with the letter **p**.

Tap the map, Mac.

Consonants Cc and Pp

 Read

 I am Cam.

 I am Pam.

 I pat the cat.

 I like the cap.

Directions Remind students that the letter *p* makes the sound /p/ and the letter *c* can make the sound /k/. Have partners take turns using letter-sound relationships to decode the VC and CVC words and read the sentences.

102

Consonants Cc and Pp

 **MY TURN** (Circle) and <u>underline</u>

I am (Pam).

I have a c̲at.

I like the cat.

I pat the cat.

Directions Remind students that the letter *p* makes the sound /p/ and the letter *c* can make the sound /k/. Have students circle the words with the letter *p* and underline the words with the letter *c*. Then have students take turns reading the sentences with a partner.

Read Together

I can read about special places.

Informational Text

Informational texts tell about real people, places, or things.

Main Idea	• There are many things at the playground.
Details	• There is a slide.
	There are swings.
	There is a sandbox.

 **TURN and TALK** Talk about how this informational text is different from a realistic fiction story.

Directions Read the genre information and model text to students. Say: The central, or main, idea of an informational text is what the text is mostly about. Supporting evidence, or details, tells more about the main idea. Have students compare and contrast the informational text and realistic fiction stories.

Informational Text
Anchor chart

Park

Main Idea

Detail

Detail

Detail

At the Library

Preview Vocabulary

library

librarian

computers

movie

Read

Read the text and look at the pictures to learn why a library is a special place.

Meet the Author

Eric Braun has written more than one hundred books, including *If I Were an Astronaut*. He lives in Minnesota with his wife, two sons, dog, and gecko.

At the Library

written by Eric Braun

 AUDIO

Audio with Highlighting

ANNOTATE

The library is a special place.
People can do many things here.

CLOSE READ

What words tell the main idea of the text? <u>Underline</u> the words.

Here are the books.
He can find a good book to read.

Here are the computers.
She can use it to tell a story.

Here are the movies.
They can take a movie home.

This is story time.
The children listen to a story.

CLOSE READ

What words tell about the main idea? Highlight the words in the text.

This is a teacher.
She helps students with
their homework.

This is the librarian.
He helps people find books.

The library is a great place!

Develop Vocabulary

 Match

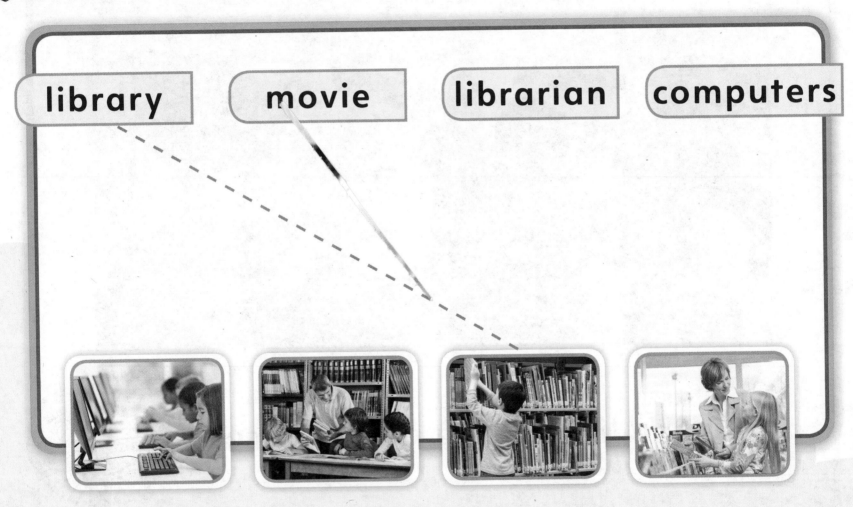

library   movie   librarian   computers

Directions Say: You can use pictures and words in a text to help you learn the meaning of a new word. Read the vocabulary words to students. Have them go back to the text and discuss the meanings of the words. Then have students use pictures to clarify the meanings of the words by drawing lines from each word to the matching picture.

116

Check for Understanding

 Write

1. One way libraries are special is

_____

- -

_____ .

2. Why did the author write this text?

_____

- -

_____

3. What does a librarian do?

_____

- -

_____

Directions Read item 1 and encourage students to write an answer. Continue with items 2 and 3. Remind students to use text evidence to support their responses.

Find Main Idea

The **central**, or **main**, **idea** is what a text is mostly about.

 (Circle) and draw

library	computer

118

Directions Read the information to students. Have them look back at the text. Ask students to circle the word that tells the main idea. Then have them draw about the main idea.

Use Text Evidence

 **Draw**

Directions Explain that text evidence is the details in a text that support, or tell about, the main idea. Say: Think about the central, or main, idea of the text. How do you know this is the main idea? Have students draw two details from the text that support their response on the previous page. Remind them to look back at the text.

Reflect and Share

 Draw

Weekly Question

What makes us want to visit a special place?

Directions Tell students they read about a library. Ask them to think of other special places they have read about. Have them respond to sources by drawing a picture of a library and another place they read about.

Read Together

I can use words to make connections.

My Learning Goal

Academic Vocabulary

map	move	land	special

 **MY TURN** Write

We use a _map_ to help us find places.

A park is a _____ place.

Directions Read the Academic Vocabulary words to students. Then read the sentences. Have students respond using newly acquired vocabulary by choosing the appropriate words to write on the lines.

121

Concept Sort

 Circle

 B  4

Directions Say: A category is a group of items that has something in common. We can name the items in a group and then say what they have in common. Have students name the three items in the boxes and identify the category as shapes. Finally, have students circle and say the picture names that belong in the category.

Read Together

Read Like a Writer, Write for a Reader

 Write

1. Find a word or group of words that tells why the author thinks libraries are special.

_____

- -

_____

2. What other word or group of words can you write to tell why libraries are special?

_____

- -

_____

Directions Read the first item to students and have them look back at the text to find an answer. Then read the second item. Ask students to write a word or group of words that tells why they think libraries are special.

Plural Nouns

We add **s** to the end of some nouns to name more than one.

1 dog

2 dogs

 Tell how many there are of each thing. Which word needs an **s** at the end?

MY TURN (Circle) and write

The two tree are tall.

_____

- -

_____

124

Directions Read the information at the top of the page. Have partners count the books and desk in the pictures and discuss which word needs a plural ending. Then read the sentence with students. Have them edit the sentence by circling the word that should end with s. Ask them to write the plural noun on the line.

I can draw or write.

My Learning Goal

Types of Books

 Write and draw

_____

- -

_____

Directions Say: Some books tell a story. Some books tell facts. Some books tell how to do something. Have students think about different types of books they have read. Then ask them to create a cover for a book. They should think of a title and a picture that shows what the book is about and what type of book it is.

Spaces Between Words

Letters make up a word.

Words make up a sentence.

There are spaces between the words in a sentence.

 (Circle)

Here are the computers.

 Write

Here	are	the	books.

126

Directions Have students recognize the difference between a letter and a word in the sentence by first naming letters they know and then pointing to each word. Ask them to circle the spaces between the words to show word boundaries. Finally, have students use the words in the word bank to write a sentence.

When to Start a New Book

Before you start a new book, make sure the book you are writing is finished. You can use a checklist.

 **MY TURN** Check

☐ Did you make a title page?

☐ Did you color the pictures?

☐ Can you add more details?

☐ Did you put spaces between the words?

Directions Discuss the items on the checklist with students. Explain that they can use the checklist to help evaluate and revise their own writing.

127

Exploring the Woods

There is a lot to see in the woods!

You can see trees.

You can see animal homes.

You can see bugs too!

128

What is fun about exploring new places?

Directions Read the text to students. Then have them interact with the source by coloring the picture. As they color, have students talk about the things they see in the woods.

Middle Sounds

 Match

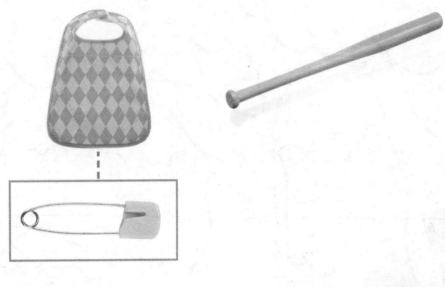

130

Directions Model: Listen to the sounds in the word *pin:* /p/ /i/ /n/. What sound is in the middle? That's right! The sound in the middle is /i/. Have students name the pictures and identify the middle sound in each word. Then ask them to draw a line from each picture word that has the medial sound /i/ to the picture of the pin.

Short i Spelled i

 Write

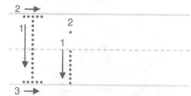

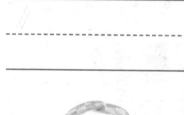

Directions Tell students that the letter *i* can make the sound /i/. Explain that they will see the letter *i* in many words with the short *i* sound. Model how to form the letters *I* and *i*. Then ask students to say the sounds in each picture word and identify the middle sound. Say: If the picture word has the sound /i/ in the middle, write the letters *Ii*.

Short i Spelled i

 **MY TURN** Read and (circle)

s i p

p i t

s i t

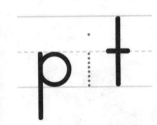

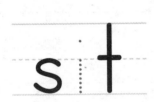

Directions Have students trace the letter *i* in each word. Then have them read the word and circle the matching picture.

Initial and Final Sounds

 SEE and SAY Circle

Directions Model: Listen to the sounds in this word: /n/ /e/ /t/, *net*. The word *net* begins with the sound /n/. Have students identify the picture words in the first row and circle the pictures that begin with the sound /n/. Then have students continue with the second row, circling picture words that end with the sound /n/.

133

Consonant Nn

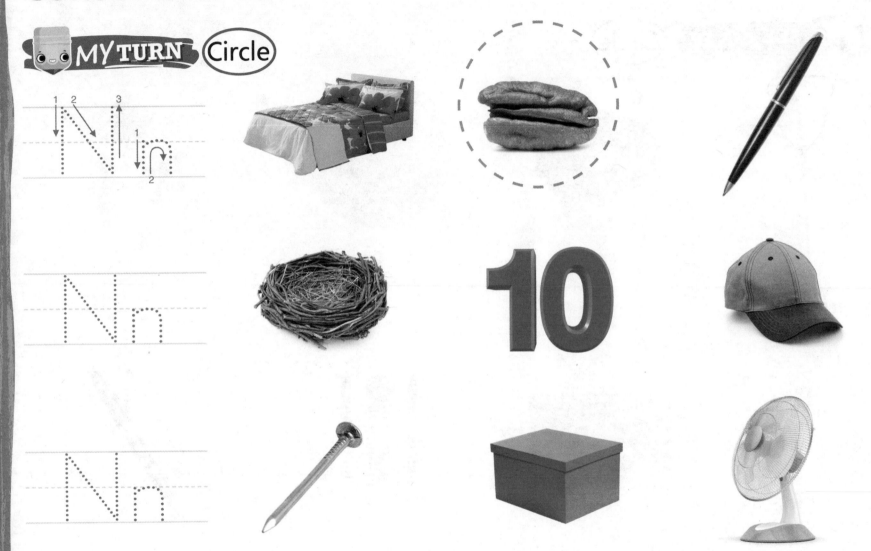

Directions Tell students that the letter *n* makes the sound /n/. Say: You will see the letter *n* in many words with the sound /n/. Model how to form the letters *N* and *n*. Have students trace the letters *Nn* in each row and identify the sound the letters make. Then have them circle the picture words that begin or end with the sound for *n*.

My Words to Know

| my | we | make |

My Sentences to Read

MY TURN

I <u>make</u> my pit in the .

We sit in it.

Directions Say: Listen as I read these words: *my, we, make*. Have students read the high-frequency words and then the sentences, using the word *dirt* to name the image. Say: Underline the high-frequency words in the sentences.

Consonant Nn

 MY TURN Write and read

n   n   n   n

Directions Have students say the name of each picture, listening to the sound /n/ in each word. Have them practice writing the letter *n*. Then have them choose two of the words to read and write on the lines.

In the Pit

Highlight the words with the short i sound.

I make a pit.

We can sit in my pit.

 AUDIO

Audio with Highlighting

ANNOTATE

137

Tim <u>can</u> tip a pan.

I can tap a pan.

Underline the words with the **n** sound.

It is a pin!

Short i and Consonant Nn

 **TURN**and**TALK** Read

pit   **tip**   **pin**

Nan   **nap**   **Nat**

pan   **tan**   **can**

sit   **Tim**   **sip**

140

Directions Say: Remember that the letter *i* can make the sound /i/ and the letter *n* makes the sound /n/. Have students take turns reading the words with a partner.

Short i and Consonant Nn

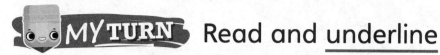 Read and <u>underline</u>

<u>sit</u>   sip

man   nap

pit   pin

pan   can

Directions Say: Remember that the letter *n* makes the sound /n/ and the letter *i* can make the sound /i/. Read each pair of words and underline the word that names the picture.

141

 **My Learning Goal** I can read realistic fiction.

SPOTLIGHT ON GENRE

Realistic Fiction

The **setting** is where and when a story takes place.

TURN and TALK Tell a partner about the setting in the picture.

142

Directions Read the information at the top of the page to students. Then have them work with a partner to describe the setting in the picture, including the time and the place.

Realistic Fiction
Anchor Chart

Place and Time

December

Sunday	Monday	Tuesday	Wednesday	Thursday	Friday	Saturday
1	2	3	4	5	6	7
8	9	10	11	12	13	14
15	16	17	18	19	20	21
22	23	24	25	26	27	28
29	30	31				

Setting

Read Together

Where Is Twister?

Preview Vocabulary

chasing	slips	scrambles	follows

Read

Read to find out who Twister is.

Meet the Author

Bonnie Lass is a teacher who writes stories for beginning readers. She is the author of *Who Took the Cookies from the Cookie Jar?*

144

Where Is Twister?

written by Bonnie Lass

illustrated by Josée Masse

AUDIO

Audio with
Highlighting

ANNOTATE

Olivia and Twister are in the barnyard.
Olivia is feeding the chickens.
Twister helps.

CLOSE READ

Where does the story take place? Underline the word.

Olivia looks up.
She thinks, "Where is Twister?"
Twister is chasing a butterfly!

147

Twister stops. Where is he?
Twister is in the woods!

148

CLOSE READ

What detail does the text tell about the woods? Highlight the words.

There are lots of sticks here.
Twister finds a good one to chew on.

149

Chewing makes Twister thirsty.
He finds a creek and has a drink.

Copyright © SAVVAS Learning Company LLC. All Rights Reserved.

Twister slips and falls in!
Twister is scared.

Twister scrambles out.
He shakes himself dry
in the sunshine.
Look! There is the butterfly!

CLOSE READ

When does the story take place? Underline the clue.

Twister follows the butterfly home.
"Twister!" says Olivia.
"You came back to me!"

Develop Vocabulary

 **MY TURN** Write

| slips | follows | chasing | scrambles |

Twister starts _____ a butterfly.

Directions Say: The words and pictures in a text can help you learn and understand the meaning of a word. Have students look back at the text and discuss the meanings of the vocabulary words. Then have them identify the word that best completes the sentence. Ask them to write the word on the lines.

Check for Understanding

 Write

1. What happens at the end of the story?

_____

- -

_____

2. What words help you know how Olivia feels?

_____

- -

_____

3. Do you think Twister will go back into the woods?

_____

- -

_____

Directions Read the questions and have students write their responses. Remind them to use evidence from the text.

Describe Setting

 **MY TURN** (Circle) and write

The **setting** is where and when a story takes place.

_____

- - - - - - - - - - - - - - - - - - - -

_____

156

Directions Read aloud the information and ask students to circle the picture that shows the setting at the beginning of the story. Remind them to look back at the text. Then have students write words that describe when and where the story takes place on the lines.

Create New Understandings

You can use details you learn in a story to understand something new.

 **MY TURN** Draw

Directions Read the information to students. Have them synthesize information from the story to draw the woods setting. Remind students to look back at the text. Ask: What did you learn about the woods that you did not know before?

Reflect and Share

 TURN and TALK What is the setting of the story?
What other stories have you read that have a similar
setting? Talk about the stories.

Weekly Question

What is fun about exploring new places?

158

Directions Ask students to talk about the setting in the story. Then ask them to respond to sources by talking
with a partner about other stories they have read that take place in a similar setting.

Read Together

I can use words to tell about stories.

My Learning Goal

Academic Vocabulary

map	move	land	special

Word parts can be added to words to make new words.

 Underline

The plane <u>landed</u> on the ground.

Tim moves fast.

Directions Say: A word part can change the meaning of a word. The ending *-ed* tells about an action that happened in the past. The ending *-s* tells about an action that is happening now. Read the sentences and have students underline the word in each sentence that has a word part added to it.

159

Concept Sort

Directions Say: A category is a group of items that has something in common. We can say the items and then identify, or name, the category. Have students name what they see in the three boxes and then identify the category: colors. Then have students circle the pictures in each row that are the same color. Have them talk about other words that would fit in the category.

Read Like a Writer, Write for a Reader

 Write

1. Find a word in the text that helps you imagine how Twister feels when he falls into the creek.

_____

- -

_____

2. What word can you write to help readers picture Twister?

_____

- -

_____

Directions Say: We can experience a story by picturing it in our minds. Read aloud pp. 150–151 as students picture the events in their minds. Then read the first item to students and have them write their answer on the lines. Continue with the second item. Have students discuss their answers.

Plural Nouns

We add **es** to some nouns to name more than one.

branch

branches

 Write

peach

peach _____

Directions Read to students the information at the top of the page. Then have students read the words. Tell them to edit the word *peach* by changing it to its plural form to match the picture.

Read Together

I can draw or write.

My Learning Goal

Writing Club

What will you do in Writing Club?

1. You will share your writing.

2. You will talk about your writing.

3. You will listen to others' ideas.

TURN and TALK Introduce yourself to your small group. Then talk about what you want to write about.

Writing Club will help make you a better writer!

Directions Have students develop social communication by introducing themselves using common greetings. Then ask them to practice sharing with others by telling what they want to write about. **Model:** Hello, my name is [name]. I want to write about my trip to the lake.

Ask and Answer Questions

 Draw

 TURN and TALK Answer questions your group asks about your drawing. Ask questions about their drawings.

164

Directions Have students draw about a topic or event. Then ask them to describe their drawing to a small group. Encourage students to ask and answer questions to clarify understanding. Remind them to listen actively to others and to take turns speaking.

Make and Respond to Suggestions

 Draw

 **TURN and TALK** Share your ideas about your partner's drawing. Listen to your partner's ideas about your drawing.

Directions Say: Sharing and listening to ideas about what we write helps make our writing better. Have students draw a special place and then show their drawing to a partner. Have partners discuss ways they can make their drawings better, such as adding details. Remind them to take turns speaking.

What Is in a Neighborhood?

A map shows where places and things are. What special places do you see?

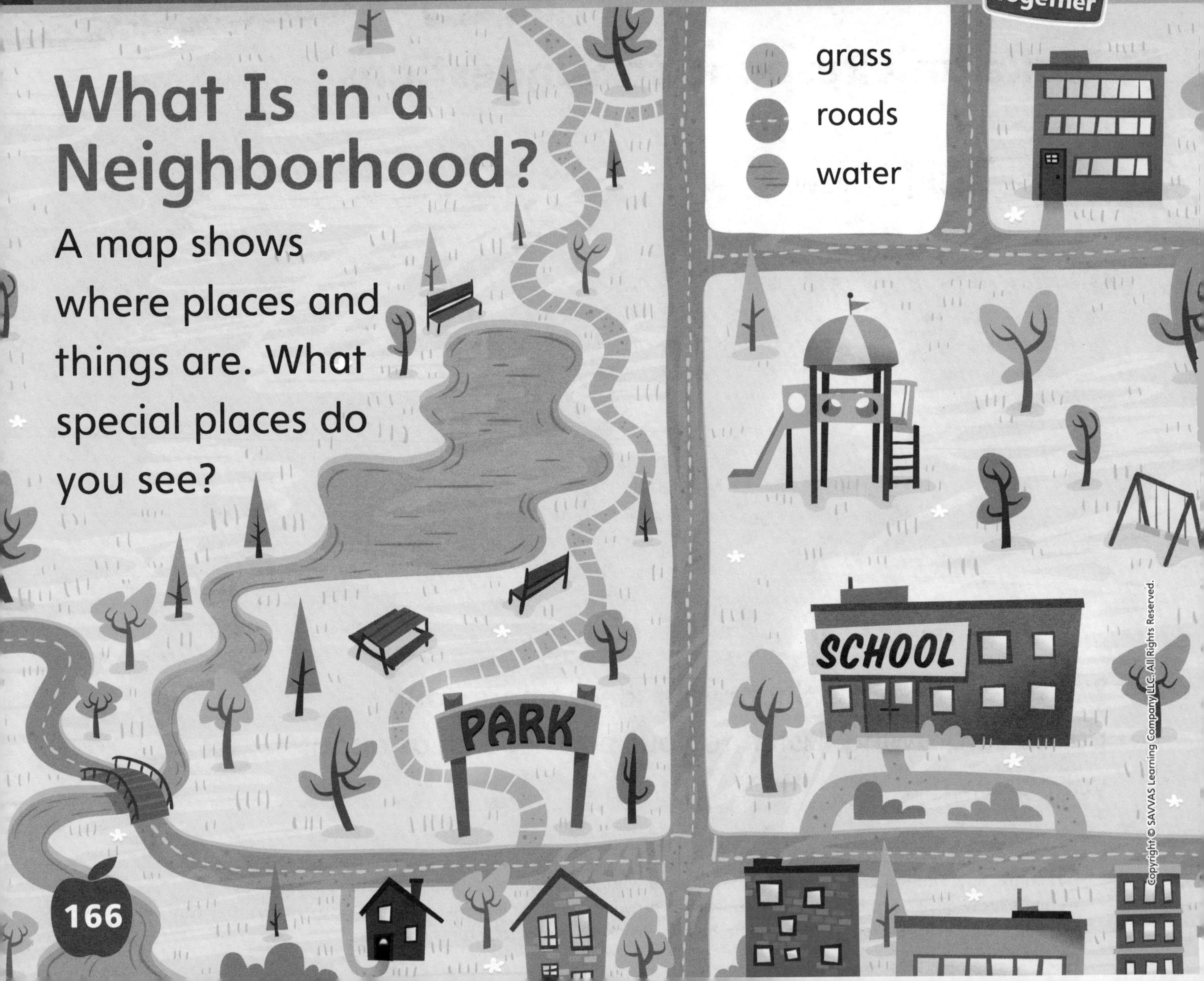

grass
roads
water

PARK

SCHOOL

Consonant Bb

MY TURN Circle

Directions Tell students that the letter *b* makes the sound /b/. Say: You will see the letter *b* in many words with the sound /b/. Model how to form the letters *B* and *b*. Then have students identify and circle each uppercase *B* and lowercase *b* in the letter jumble. As they circle a letter, ask them to say the sound the letter represents and then trace *B* or *b* on the lines.

169

Consonant Bb

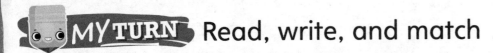 Read, write, and match

 bin

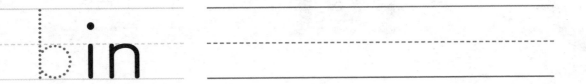 bit

 bat

170

Directions Have students trace the letter *b* in each word. Then have them read the words and write them on the lines. Finally, have students draw a line from each word to the matching picture.

Initial Sounds

 Circle

Directions Have students say each picture word and circle the items whose names begin with /r/. Model: Listen to this word: *rock*. I hear the sound /r/ at the beginning of *rock*.

Consonant Rr

 Circle

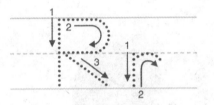

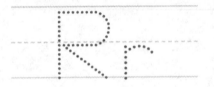

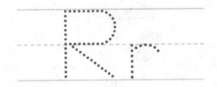

172

Directions Tell students that the letter *r* makes the sound /r/. Explain that they will see the letter *r* in many words with the sound /r/. Model how to form the letters *R* and *r*. Say: Name the pictures in each row and circle the picture word that begins with the sound /r/. Name the letter that makes the sound. Then trace the letters on the lines.

My Words to Know

me	for	with

My Sentences to Read

Sit <u>with</u> me.

He can bat for me.

Directions Say: Listen as I read these words: *me, for, with*. Have students read the high-frequency words. Then have them read the sentences and identify the high-frequency words by underlining them.

Consonant Rr

 Read and write

r

r

r

174

Directions Have students name each picture and trace the letter *r*. Have them write the words on the lines and read them.

Ric at Bat

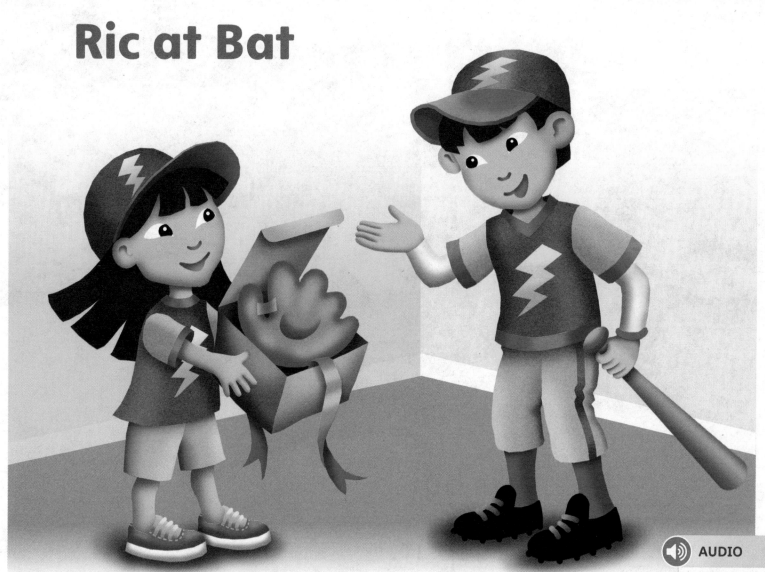

AUDIO

Audio with Highlighting

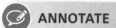

ANNOTATE

The mitt is for me!

175

Ric is at bat.

He can rip it.

Can I nab it with my mitt?

176

Highlight the words with the **r** sound.

Underline the words with the **b** sound.

Ric ran. I sat.

177

Consonants Rr and Bb

 **MY TURN** Write and read

rip

rib

bin

bit

bat

rat

178

Directions Have students trace each initial *r* or *b*. Ask them to point to the letters that are different in each pair of words. Then have students decode each word.

Consonants Rr and Bb

 **MY TURN** (Circle, underline, and match

I like to (rip).

The cat <u>bit</u> it.

He ran with me.

I have a bat.

Directions Have students read each sentence, underlining words that begin with *b* and circling words that begin with *r*. Then have them match each sentence to the picture that illustrates it.

Read
Together

My Learning Goal

I can read about special places.

Informational Text

The purpose of informational texts is to inform.

Purpose → Let me tell you about the library.

Facts → The library has a lot of books.

We do not buy books at a library. We borrow them.

 TURN *and* **TALK** Discuss how a story about a library would be different from the informational text.

Directions Read the genre information and the model text to students. Ask them to discuss the purpose of the text. Then have partners contrast a story about a library with the model text.

Informational Text
Anchor Chart

Purpose: to inform about a topic

Fact

Fact

Topic: Cats

Facts tell information about the topic.

Fact

Fact

A Visit to the Art Store

Preview Vocabulary

tools

pencils

brushes

markers

Read

Read the text and look at the pictures to learn about why people go to art stores.

Meet the Author

Jerry Craft has written or drawn pictures for lots of books, including a superhero book that he wrote with his two sons. He also does a newspaper comic strip, and he loves to do school visits!

A Visit to the Art Store

by Jerry Craft

AUDIO

Audio with Highlighting

ANNOTATE

Do you want to be an artist?
An art store has the tools you need.

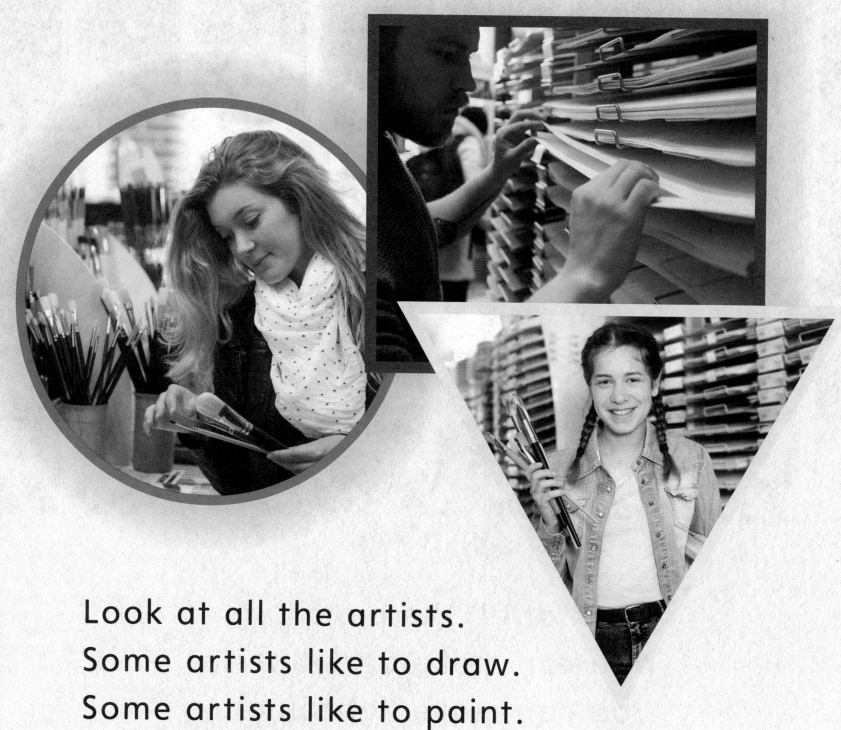

Look at all the artists.
Some artists like to draw.
Some artists like to paint.

Look at all the pencils.
You can make dark lines.
You can make light lines.

CLOSE READ

What does the author tell us we can do with art supplies? <u>Underline</u> things we can do.

Look at all the markers.
You can use every color of the rainbow.

187

Look at all the paints.
You can use bright colors.
You can use dull colors.

CLOSE READ

What does the author tell us we can do with art supplies? <u>Underline</u> things we can do.

Look at all the brushes.
You can use wide brushes.
You can use thin brushes.

Shopping for art supplies can be
a lot of fun.

CLOSE READ

What words tell why people go to the art store? Highlight the words.

But using art supplies is even more fun!

191

Develop Vocabulary

 Circle

brushes (markers)

brushes   pencils

tools   brushes

markers   pencils

Directions Read the words below each picture to students. Have them circle the word that names the picture.

Read
Together

Check for Understanding

 **MY TURN** Write

1. This text is mostly about

_____

- -

_____.

2. What words help you picture making art with paint?

_____

- -

_____

3. What other tools might you find at an art store?

_____

- -

_____

Directions Read the items and have students write their answers. Remind them to use text evidence to support their responses.

Discuss Author's Purpose

The **author's purpose** is the reason an author has for writing.

 Circle

to entertain   to inform

194

Directions Read aloud the information at the top of the page. Have students discuss why the author wrote the text and circle the author's purpose. Then have them circle details from the text that support the author's purpose. Remind students to look back at the text.

Make Connections

 Draw

Directions Say: We can connect the ideas we read about with our own community. Have students make connections to society by drawing one reason people might visit an art store in their community. Remind them to look back at the text.

Reflect and Share

 TURN and TALK What makes an art store a special place? What makes a library a special place? Tell details from the texts.

You can retell important details.

Weekly Question

How can we describe special places?

Directions Tell students they read about art stores. Remind them they have also read about libraries. Have partners respond to sources by retelling the texts. Say: When you retell a text, you tell the most important ideas and details.

Read Together

I can use words to make connections.

My Learning Goal

Academic Vocabulary

map	move	land	special

 Draw

 Talk with a partner about your drawing.

Directions Have students choose a word that they learned in this unit and draw a picture about the word. Then have them talk with a partner about what they drew and why.

Concept Sort

 Sort

Directions Say: Some of these pictures show toys, and some show objects that are not toys. Sort the pictures by putting the toys in the toy box. Have students draw lines from the pictures of toys to the empty box at the bottom of the page.

Read Like a Writer, Write for a Reader

MY TURN (Circle) and write

1. Circle the picture that helped you learn more about art stores.

2. How can adding pictures help you as an author?

_____

_____

_____

_____

Directions Read item 1 to students and have them circle the picture that shows details about an art store. Then read aloud item 2 and have students write their response.

199

 **Read Together**

Singular and Plural Nouns

A **singular noun** names one.

A **plural noun** names more than one.

See the pencil and brush.

See the pencil**s** and brush**es**.

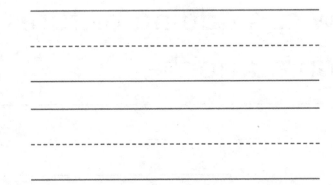

 **MY TURN** (Circle) and write

I have one dog and two cat.

She has three fox.

200

Directions Read the information and example sentences to students. Then have students edit the sentences at the bottom of the page. Ask them to circle the words that need a plural ending and write the plural nouns on the lines. Have them identify the singular noun in the sentences.

I can draw or write.

Edit for Parts of a Book

A book has a **front cover**, a **back cover**, and a **title page**.

 Write

_____   _____   _____

- - - - - - - - - - - - -   - - - - - - - - - - - - -   - - - - - - - - - - - - -

_____   _____   _____

Directions Tell students that the front cover names the title and author of a book, the title page is the first page in the book and also names the title and author, and the back cover tells details about the book. Then ask students to identify the front cover, back cover, and title page by writing the correct term below each picture.

Incorporate Peer Feedback

 Draw

Directions Have students talk with a partner about the picture and take turns suggesting details they can add to make it better. Then ask students to work independently to revise the picture by adding details. Encourage them to include details their partner suggested.

How to Celebrate

- ☐ Speak loudly and clearly.
- ☐ Use complete sentences.
- ☐ Listen actively.
- ☐ Ask questions.

TURN and TALK Share your writing with a partner.

Directions Discuss the list of speaking and listening rules with students. Then have them share their writing with a partner.

UNIT THEME

Going Places

 **TURN***and***TALK**

Go back to each text and tell one detail about a special place. Use the Weekly Questions to help you.

BOOK CLUB

WEEK 3

At the Library

What makes us want to visit a special place?

WEEK 2

Too Many Places to Hide

What is exciting about moving to a new place?

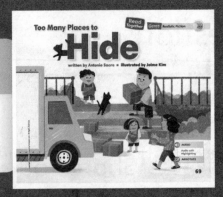

BOOK CLUB

WEEK 1

Mission Accomplished!

How does imagination make a place seem different?

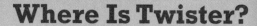

BOOK CLUB

Where Is Twister?

What is fun about exploring new places?

WEEK 4

BOOK CLUB

WEEK 5

A Visit to the Art Store

How can we describe special places?

BOOK CLUB

Essential Question

What makes a place special?

Project

WEEK 6

Now it is time to apply what you learned about going places in your **WEEK 6 PROJECT: Let's Go!**

205

Short a Word Families

 **Write**

pan

cat

206

Directions Have students say the word for each picture and segment the sounds before writing the word on the lines. **Model:** Listen to the sounds in *pan:* /p/ /a/ /n/. The letter for /p/ is *p*. The letter for /a/ is *a*. The letter for /n/ is *n*.

My Words to Know

she	see	look

My Sentences to Read

1. I <u>see</u> Nat.

2. She is at the mat.

3. Look! It is in the can!

Directions Have students read the high-frequency words and then the sentences. Ask them to underline the high-frequency words in the sentences.

Short i Word Families

 Write

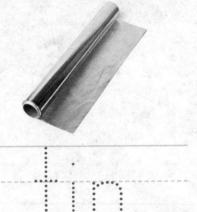

i n

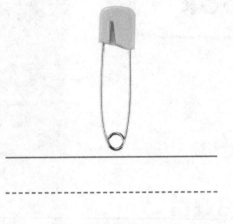

_____

_____

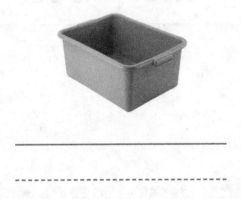

_____

_____

t i p

_____

_____

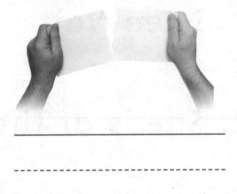

_____

_____

Directions Have students say the word for each picture and segment the sounds before writing the word on the lines.

We Like It!

Highlight the words that are in the same word family as **fin**.

Tim can see a pin.

Look! It is in the bin.

 AUDIO

Audio with Highlighting

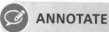 **ANNOTATE**

209

Pat can <u>tap</u> with a bat.

She can rap with Nat.

<u>Underline</u> words that are in the same word family as **cap**.

We sit for a nap.

Let's Go!

Look at the pictures. Which type of museum do you want to go to?

 **COLLABORATE** Talk about museums.

212

Directions Read aloud the prompt. Say: A museum is a place where interesting things are collected for people to see. Have students discuss the museums in the pictures and what people can see at the museums. Then have students circle the museums they have visited or museums they would like to visit.

Use Words

COLLABORATE What questions can you ask about museums? Talk with your partner. Use new academic words.

Museum Research Plan

Check each box as you do your work.

☐ Research the museums.

☐ Choose which one you want to go to.

☐ Draw or write to tell why.

☐ Share with others.

Directions Have students generate questions about museums using newly acquired vocabulary. Then discuss the steps in this week's research plan. Explain that students will follow the research plan as they complete their project.

Read Together

Fact and Opinion

A **fact** is a detail that can be proved to be true.

An **opinion** is what the author thinks or feels.

You should go to a history museum!

You can see dinosaurs.

214

Directions Say: The author of an opinion text wants to convince readers to think or do something. The author tells an opinion. The author uses facts to support the opinion. Read the sentences below the pictures to students. Have them circle the sentence that tells a fact and underline the sentence that tells an opinion.

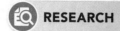

Ask a Librarian

🔍 RESEARCH

You can find information in a library.

A librarian can help you!

COLLABORATE Circle who can help you in a library. Talk about questions you can ask.

Directions Say: What do you want to know about your topic? Think of questions you can ask. Asking librarians questions helps them know what you need and want. For example, say, *Hello. Where may I find books about museums?* Have students circle the librarian in the picture. Then have them generate questions for their inquiry project. Tell them to express their needs and wants.

Take Notes

What can you see?

You can learn about animals from the past.

 COLLABORATE Draw what you can see at each museum.

Directions Discuss the research model with students. Say: You can gather, or get, information about art and history museums by looking at books. Have students gather information from a variety of books about art and history museums. Ask them to draw notes about what they can see at each type of museum.

Tell Your Opinion

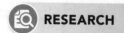 RESEARCH

You can draw and write to tell your opinion.

 COLLABORATE Circle the museum you like better.

 COLLABORATE Draw

Directions Remind students that an opinion is what they think or feel about a topic. Read aloud the information and have students circle the picture that shows the type of museum they would rather visit. Then have them draw a picture to show what they learned about the museum they chose.

Share

Follow the rules for speaking and listening.

Reflect

Did I work well with others?

Did I like my project?

 218

Directions Say: You can share your project in different ways. You can show your writing, talk about your project, and show pictures. **Tell students to choose an appropriate mode of delivery to present their project. Then have them reflect on their project by answering the questions.**

Reflect on Your Reading

 Write

I think

Reflect on Your Writing

 Write

My favorite writing is

Directions Have students share their ideas about their reading and writing.

How to Use a Picture Dictionary

school

This is a picture of the word.

This is the word you are learning.

 Draw

220

Directions Say: You can use a picture dictionary to find words. The words are grouped into topics. The topic of this picture dictionary is **locations**. Listen as I read the words. The pictures will help you understand the meanings of the words. Have students identify the word *farm* in the picture dictionary and use it in a sentence. Then have them draw a picture of what the word means.

Locations

playground

farm

city

home

store

How to Use a Glossary

The word is in dark type.

Cc   **circle** A **circle** is a perfectly round line.

All words that begin with the letter C will be after Cc.

This sentence will help you understand what the word means.

 **MY TURN** Draw

Directions Say: A glossary can help you find the meanings of words you do not know. The words in a glossary are in alphabetical, or ABC, order. Have students find the word *tools* and draw a picture of the word.

Bb

brushes **Brushes** are tools used for painting.

Cc

chasing When you are **chasing** something, you are running after it to catch it.

circle A **circle** is a perfectly round line.

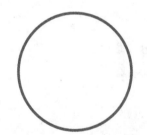

computers **Computers** are electronic machines.

crawls Someone who **crawls** moves on his or her hands and knees.

cube A **cube** is a solid object with six square sides.

Ff

follows When someone **follows** something, he or she goes after it.

Ll

land **Land** is the solid part of the earth's surface.

librarian A **librarian** is a person who helps at a library.

library A **library** is a place where books and other things are kept for people to borrow.

Mm

map A **map** is a drawing that shows where things are located.

markers **Markers** are tools with colorful ink used for writing or drawing.

move When you **move**, you change the place where you live.

movie A **movie** is a story that is told with moving pictures.

Pp

peeks When someone **peeks**, he or she looks quickly at someone or something.

pencils **Pencils** are pointed tools used for writing or drawing.

plunks When someone **plunks** something down, he or she sets it down hard.

Ss

scrambles When someone **scrambles**, he or she moves or climbs quickly.

slips Someone who **slips** loses his or her balance and slides.

special When something is **special**, it is very important.

square A **square** is a shape with four equal sides.

Tt

tools **Tools** are objects a person uses to do a job or activity.

triangle A **triangle** is a shape with three sides and three corners.

Uu

unpacks When someone **unpacks**, he or she takes things out of a container.

Photographs

Photo locators denoted as follows Top (T), Center (C), Bottom (B), Left (L), Right (R), Background (Bkgd)

6 Shalom Ormsby/Blend Images/Getty Images; 7 Soleg/iStock/Getty Images Plus/Getty Images; 8 (BL) Dmitry Bruskov/Shutterstock, (Bkgd) Suzanne Tucker/Shutterstock; 9 (T) Shalom Ormsby/Blend Images/Getty Images, (B) Soleg/iStock/Getty Images Plus/Getty Images; 10 Umarazak/Shutterstock; 13 Chuyuss/Shutterstock; 14 (BL) Sean Locke Photography/Shutterstock, (C) Macrovector/ Shutterstock, (CL) Sean Locke Photography/Shutterstock, (T) Aphelleon/Shutterstock, (TR) Alex Mit/Shutterstock; 15 (BR) Monkey Business Images/Shutterstock, (TL) Sergeydv/123RF; 16 (BCL) Eurobanks/Shutterstock, (BCR) Tritooth/123RF, (BL) Triff/ Shutterstock, (BR) Steshkin Yevgeniy/Shutterstock, (TCL) Deep OV/ Shutterstock, (TCR) Igor Terekhov/123RF, (TL) Tsekhmister/ Shutterstock, (TR) Africa Studio/Shutterstock; 17 (BC) Carolina K. Smith MD/Shutterstock, (BL) Threeseven/Shutterstock, (BR) Kiri11/ Shutterstock, (C) Ludmilafoto/Shutterstock, (CL) Apopium/Fotolia, (CR) Pakowacz/Shutterstock, (TC) Everything/Shutterstock, (TL) Eurobanks/Shutterstock, (TR) Everything/Shutterstock; 18 (BR) Eric Isselee/Shutterstock, (TL) Tsekhmister/Shutterstock, (TR) Stockagogo/Craig Barhorst/Shutterstock, (BL) Africa Studio/ Shutterstock; 19 (BL) Domnitsky/Shutterstock, (BR) Lisa A. Svara/ Shutterstock, (TCL) Philipimage/Shutterstock, (TCR) Vitalii Tiahunov/123RF, (TL) Tarasov/Shutterstock, (TR) Africa Studio/ Shutterstock; 20 (BC) DenisNata/Shutterstock, (BL) Triff/ Shutterstock, (BR) Igor Terekhov/123RF, (TC) Bluehand/ Shutterstock, (TL) Pongsakorn Chaina/Shutterstock, (TR) Africa Studio/Shutterstock; 22 (BC) 123RF, (BL) Eric Isselee/Shutterstock, (BR) Robyn Mackenzie/123RF, (TC) Sergio Schnitzler/Shutterstock, (TL) Philipimage/Shutterstock, (TR) Nick Biebach/123RF; 26 (BR) Pakhnyushcha/Shutterstock, (BL) Philipimage/Shutterstock, (BC) Pongsakorn Chaina/Shutterstock, (TC) Eurobanks/Shutterstock, (TR) Africa Studio/Shutterstock, (TL) Pakowacz/Shutterstock; 27 (TR) Eric Isselee/Shutterstock, (BR) Tsekhmister/Shutterstock, (BCR) Eric Isselee/Shutterstock, (TCR) Arogant/Shutterstock; 45 (BR) BCFC/ Shutterstock, (CR) Voyagerix/Shutterstock; 46 (BC) Triff/ Shutterstock, (TR) 123RF, (TC) Eric Isselee/Shutterstock, (TL) Roblan/123RF; 48 (L) 123RF, (R) Lisa A. Svara/Shutterstock; 50 (BCL) Monkey Business Images/Shutterstock, (BCR) Wavebreakmedia/

Shutterstock, (BL) Racorn/Shutterstock, (BR) Rob Marmion/ Shutterstock; 52 (T) Johavel/Shutterstock, (CR) Zoonar GmbH/Alamy Stock Photo, (BL) OJO Images Ltd/Alamy Stock Photo; 53 (R) 123RF, (C) Monkey Business Images/Shutterstock, (L) Anna Krestiannykova/ Shutterstock; 54 (BCL) Morena Valente/Shutterstock, (BCR) Tim Large/Shutterstock, (BL) DenisNata/Shutterstock, (TCR) Alex Staroseltsev/Shutterstock, (TL) Lisovskaya Natalia/Shutterstock, (TR) Paul Orr/Shutterstock, (TCL) Everything/Shutterstock, (BR) Lisa A. Svara/Shutterstock; 55 (BL) Room27/Shutterstock, (BR) Deep OV/ Shutterstock, (CL) Apopium/Fotolia, (CR) Eric Isselee/Shutterstock, (TL) Thomas Soellner/Shutterstock, (TR) Eurobanks/Shutterstock; 56 (BL) DenisNata/Shutterstock, (CL) Anton Starikov/123RF, (TL) Pakowacz/Shutterstock; 57 (BCL) Africa Studio/Shutterstock, (BCR) Morenina/Shutterstock, (BL) Sergiy1975/Shutterstock, (BR) Dny3d/ Shutterstock, (TCL) Adisa/Shutterstock, (TCR) Number 650371/ Shutterstock, (TL) Triff/Shutterstock, (TR) Africa Studio/ Shutterstock; 58 (BC) Morena Valente/Shutterstock, (BL) Bluehand/ Shutterstock, (BR) Phant/Shutterstock, (C) Roblan/123RF, (CL) Triff/ Shutterstock, (CR) Kirsanov Valeriy Vladimirovich/Shutterstock, (TC) Ruslan Semichev/Shutterstock, (TL) Ivaschenko Roman/Shutterstock, (TR) Sergey Peterman/Shutterstock; 60 (C) Blaj Gabriel/Shutterstock, (T) Oliver Hoffmann/Shutterstock; 65 (T) Triff/Shutterstock, (B) Celig/Shutterstock; 83 Monkey Business Images/Shutterstock; 84 (CR) LorenzoArcobasso/Shutterstock, (TL) Alex Staroseltsev/ Shutterstock, (CL) Kiri11/Shutterstock, (TR) StudioVin/Shutterstock; 86 (BR) TinnaPong/Shutterstock, (TC) Irin-k/Shutterstock, (TR) HelloRF Zcool/Shutterstock; 90 (Bkgd) Hikrcn/123RF, (BL) Jan Miko/ Shutterstock, (BR) Sam74100/123RF, (TR) Wollertz/Shutterstock; 91 (CR) Ian Dagnall/Alamy Stock Photo, (TL) Juice Images/Alamy Stock Photo; 92 (BCL) Paul Orr/Shutterstock, (BCR) Maks Narodenko/ Shutterstock, (BL) Deep OV/Shutterstock, (BR) Eurobanks/ Shutterstock, (TCL) Nerthuz/Shutterstock, (TCR) Tarasov/ Shutterstock, (TL) Fotomaster/Fotolia, (TR) Alexander Dashewsky/ Shutterstock; 93 (BC) 123RF, (BL) Lem/Shutterstock, (BR) Ozaiachin/123RF, (TC) StudioVin/Shutterstock, (TR) Bokeh Blur Background Subject/Shutterstock, (TL) Fotomaster/Fotolia; 94 (BL) 123RF, (CL) Pakowacz/Shutterstock, (TL) Celig/Shutterstock; 95 (BCL) Adisa/Shutterstock, (BCR) Room27/Shutterstock, (BR) Danny Smythe/Shutterstock, (TCR) Deep OV/Shutterstock, (TL) Testing/ Shutterstock, (TR) Phant/Shutterstock, (BL) Everything/Shutterstock, (TCL) Lisa A. Svara/Shutterstock; 96 (BC) Deep OV/Shutterstock, (BL)